A DYNAMIC FAITH.

A DYNAMIC FAITH.

BY

RUFUS M. JONES, M.A., D. Litt.

"This is the victory—even your Faith."

THIRD EDITION.

LONDON :

HEADLEY BROTHERS,

14, BISHOPSGATE STREET WITHOUT, E.C.

—

1906.

HEADLEY BROTHERS,

PRINTERS,

LONDON; AND ASHFORD, KENT.

TO THE SWEET AND SHINING
MEMORY OF A FRIEND, NOW
IN THE HEAVENLIES, WHOSE
INSPIRATION TOUCHED THESE
PAGES.

PREFACE TO FIRST EDITION.

SPITE of the fact that this appears to be a busy and materialistic age—bent on wealth and luxury and the things of sense—it is yet true that no generation has ever been more seriously concerned with the things of the Spirit than our own. The railroad, the telegraph, the telephone, the electric car, the steamship have made a new commercial world in our century. The scientific researches of the same period have given us a new universe, and made the mediæval conceptions of the world for ever unthinkable. But the supreme feature of this period is, after all, to be found in the increased vitality of religion and in the onward sweep of the Truth. There has not been a discovery recorded in all this rich period which has not sooner or later forced us to ask : How does this affect our conception of God, or what does it mean in terms of ethical and spiritual life, or how does it bear on the end-

less destiny of Man ? Every thoughtful individual
has been compelled to face the great issues of
life and death, and to adjust himself to the
march of thought. The problems of the spiritual
life have ceased to be problems exclusively for
priest and churchman : they now concern every
man who asks questions of the universe, and
they must be settled by each man for himself.
This all involves the further fact that no man
can settle down under the comfortable lee of
some ancient "authority" and *so* keep the faith.
One might as well expect to keep the beautiful
crystal of a snowflake in his warm hand. Faith
is kept, as life is kept, by constant adjustment
to environment.   Faith is, any way, but another
name for the activity and life of the inward
man. Dynamic, we have called it, but we hardly
mean more by the term than *vital, efficient, result
producing.* We have endeavoured to indicate that
faith is a spiritual process of *testing the validity*
of things unseen, and of *appreciating their worth.*
This little book deals with some aspects of such
a faith, and illustrates it through types largely
chosen from those who have proved the reality
of this spiritual process. Two of the chapters
deal with a phase of religious thought called
"Quakerism," but we trust there is no sectarian
bias in it, and we have aimed to express in a

simple way some truths which may possibly be
of profit to thoughtful Christians of all com-
munions. These papers were primarily prepared
for the "Haverford Summer School of Religious
History," and were afterwards delivered at the
Earlham Biblical Institute, Richmond, Indiana.

R. M. J.

Haverford, Pennsylvania,
    Eleventh Month, 1900.

CONTENTS.

THE BASIS OF RELIGION.

I.

THE BASIS OF RELIGION.

IT was one of the difficult, in fact, insoluble, problems of ancient philosophy to find out what supported, or held up the world. It was easy to suppose that it rested on the back of some giant creature, but then came the chilling question, What holds up your giant creature? Each answer always led to another question. The answer at last is : It rests on nothing outside itself. There is no granite foundation underneath, nor is there any giant creature. Its substance is of such a nature that it feels a mighty attraction for every particle of matter in the visible universe. The sun being the greatest body in our system exerts upon it the strongest attraction, and this invisible, intangible power or force holds it like a woven cable and swings it safely in its ellipse. We say, then, that it belongs to the nature of matter to feel an affinity for other matter, however remotely the particles may be separated, and were this not so, no means could ever be found for holding up a world in space.

There is another question which has been almost equally difficult of solution : What is the explanation, the ground, the basis of religion ? On what authority shall we build our faith ? How do we know that there is any more *reality* back of our faith than there is back of our dreams ? Then we have the common answers : God has given us a book which is an ultimate authority, and which *declares* the reality of things not seen. Or again : God has founded a church in this world by supernatural means. The founders of that church were divinely ordained and their decisions were infallibly right. They have transferred their authority to their successors and we have now in church traditions and church officials an authority which is a sure ground for faith, and which establishes the desired reality. Either of these answers will do, until someone unkindly raises the question which is sure to come sooner or later : How do we know that the Bible is God's book to us, and, if so, who is infallibly authorised to tell us what it means, in every line of it ? And secondly, what proof have we that the founders of the church were divinely ordained and possessed of infallible authority, and, if so, on what ground do we assert that their successors, or the church traditions, have such divine sanction as to make *them* authoritative ? It is the old difficulty of finding a support for our first support.— What does your giant creature stand on while he holds up the earth? It may be well to postpone our search for an external authoritative basis of religion, until we have first looked to see whether there be anything within man himself, and in his relationships, which accounts for religion. If we start with a nature totally foreign to God, an insulated personality, windowless for light from Him, and incapable of recognising such light if it did come—then it is hard to see how man could ever have any immediate certainty of a divine reality, or where we could find a reasonable basis for religion. If God could not and did not have a witness to Himself within our human spirits it is difficult to see how we could ever expect to establish the reality of His being, or have any sustained assurance of His love. We give up the problem of squaring the circle because we now know enough about the problem to know that it cannot be solved. It may as confidently be asserted that a God who is not self-revealing, who has no relationship with human spirits, who does not have a witness in human consciousness, could never be found, and the search for a basis of religion on those conditions would of necessity have to be given up. The entire agnosticism of our time grows out of the fact that thoughtful men have discovered the hopelessness of finding God either in or back of the phenomena of nature. It is now clear that no increase of either microscope or telescope will ever show Him. Push back as far as ever we may, we find

only forces, no God.   This is the fact that made
William Watson say :

> "The God I never once behold,
> Above the cloud, beneath the clod,
> The unknown God, the unknown God."

They are all looking for Him where He could not
possibly be found. In a different path lies our
true search for the "Holy Grail." The essential
fact of religion is love, and love is impossible
apart from relationships. Until two spirits can
meet, and, in some degree, understand and appreciate each other, there can be no love. It begins
with spiritual interrelation. The cloud and the
clod are mere describable phenomena ; they can
be reduced to exact description. *Love* is forever
*in*describable. It is felt and appreciated, or it
remains unknown. The moment, therefore, we get
beyond the traditional God, who is external and
one "thing" among many things, as was the case,
for instance, among the Greeks, we must not
expect to find Him apart from spiritual relationships. It is in our consciousness of His love, in
our appeal from our limited self to His infinite self,
in that unmistakeable, though indescribable, sense
that we are interrelated parts of one Self who
loves us, and who enfolds us, that a religion of
any worth becomes possible. We know, when we
love a human soul, that we can transcend our
bodily isolation, our physical insularity, and that
our spirit can share its life with another spirit.
But no description of love could ever account for

this, or be the basis of it, for souls who could not themselves so share and appreciate each other. So, too, there could be no religion of this higher sort, and the agnostics would be right, were it not for the fact—the supreme fact—that the divine Spirit and the human spirit come together and have spiritual relations together and witness to each other. Our religion—any religion on a high level—begins with the fact that it belongs to the essential life of God to impart Himself, to give Himself in love, in sympathy and in fellowship, and to share His life with men ; and with the secondary fact that we are capable of appreciating such love when we see it and of responding to it.

We start out, then, boldly, with this primary fact that there is no necessary dualism between men and God—between the divine Spirit and human spirits. Their natures are not foreign and unrelated. There is but one possible separation between them, namely, sin, which, like a cataract destroys vision, not the light, and which, once removed, leaves the two spirits face to face. God and the human spirit belong together, in as real a sense as the light and the eye do, or beauty and the artist's soul, or harmony and the musician's ear. Who ever felt the necessity of proof that the sun was shining ? In fact it makes itself known through closed lids. What greater proof could there be than that we see it ? How could you ever prove to a tone-deaf man that Beethoven's symphonies are beautiful, or to a colour-blind man

that a sunset sky is glorious? There is no convincing authority; there can be no convincing
authority beyond this appeal to consciousness.
This appeal to consciousness carries conviction and
wins *assent* because the human spirit has a capacity for truth, because it is not wholly foreign in
nature to Him who is the truth. As we come
into this world so furnished in the structure of our
mind that we must view all objects "in space"
and all events "in time," so also we come with
souls capable of recognising truth and of responding to love and of assenting to righteousness when
they present themselves; otherwise we never could
learn to prize such things. It is with this in
mind that Pascal explains religion in the famous
words: "Thou wouldst not seek me if thou hadst
not already found me." The basis of religion, on
the human side, is to be sought therefore in the
nature of the human spirit itself; in its ability to
respond to God because of a kinship to Him; in
its capacity for truth and righteousness and its
power of recognising them as such; in the
possibility of heart-purity, so that God may be
spiritually *perceived* and known, and finally, in that
act of choice and co-operation by which the
human soul becomes transformed into a divine
likeness and may attain to a union of self with the
Father of Spirits. These facts—and without them
there is no explanation of religion—will enable us
now to find a basis for faith, for revelation, for
church authority, for the communion and fellow-

ship of saints and for the ground that religion is an endless characteristic of man—as sure to abide as consciousness is.

Truth can be transferred from one person to another, or from a book to a person, only as the ideas conveyed become appropriated and assimilated in the spiritual intelligence of the recipient. The thing is not true for me until *it is seen to be* truth, until my mind grasps it and knows it to be true. Even a divine communication could be recognised as truth only after it had been taken up into a spiritual intelligence and the consciousness had responded to it. This immediate response of the human spirit to the truth when it comes is the only possible ground of certitude—but it is stronger, not weaker, than our knowledge of historic facts and events.

Whatever comes from God to us and is expressed in human terms must come through human capacity and must bear traces of human imperfection. So only could any revelation be put to human uses. Suppose a new revelation to be to-day dropped into our world from the very hand of God, with no human touch upon it. The first question would be, "How do we know it is from God?" and our answer would be, "Because it accords with our conception of Him." Then our second question would be, "What does it mean?" And at once we should begin to interpret it in human terms and apply it to human uses. Every truth, come whence it may, falls into human custody, and becomes, however divine in origin, inextricably mixed with human elements. Even God could show Himself to us only in human terms. Until men are infinite in capacity, there never can be a revelation which is an infallible authority. The man, who perhaps of all mere men was the greatest medium of revelation the world has ever seen, says with truth, "We have this treasure in earthen vessels." The *seer*, then, can never literally convey his revelation unchanged into our minds ; the best he can do is to qualify us to see for ourselves. The supreme test, therefore, of a revelation is the degree to which it *opens our eyes to what is or to what ought to be*. The whole question of the inspiration of the Scriptures turns on this other question, "Do they inspire their reader and do they come to him with a message which appeals to the highest in him?" The only biblical definition of inspiration which we have is this, that "God spoke through holy men, who were moved." This means that the "holy men" were capable of apprehending divine truth and of expressing it in human terms. They came to such a spiritual condition that they *saw*. There is nothing here contrary to human nature. It is just what we should expect from what we have already seen. When a mathematician has learned the fundamental nature of the figures of space and their relation he comes at last to see the whole curve involved in the small arc and he finds the new planet because he sees that it *must be* there.

So the man who has obeyed his heavenly visions, who has been crowding his old self out by the spiritual method of forming a new life within,— who at length has taken degrees in the divine school,—sees truth because now he has an organ to see it with. He is not less of a man, but rather more of one. God does not use him as a telephone to talk through, or as a caligraph to write through, or as a passive window to send light through, or as a stringed instrument to send music through. He uses him because he is a *holy man* who can grasp spiritual truth, and put it into human terms. He "moves upon" him, and the holy man apprehends what the moving means. The message does not come apart from his personality but through it, otherwise any other man would do for the communication as well as a holy man.

Revelation, then, cannot all be on a single level. It depends for its height wholly upon the person through whom it comes, as the same breath through a flute gives a high note or a low note, according to the stop that is fingered. If this be so—and it is hard to see how any other view could be held—then the thing we are to look for in a revelation is not infallibility, not a dictated word, but a divine message spoken through a human personality, tested in a personal life and preserved for our use to-day because it has proved its supreme worth through all the siftings of the ages.

No process of canonization, no declaration of infallibility would add to the spiritual content of a Biblical book which did not of itself speak to human needs, or bear a living message to the heart of man, nor could any conclusion of scholarship touching origin or source or date destroy or lessen the spiritual meaning or the intrinsic value of a book which does come to man with such a message. The ultimate test—in fact the only real test—of the divine quality of Scripture will always be its effect upon its readers. The human heart never has given up and it never will give up anything which could pass the supreme test of *worth*. Prove that mother love had its first origin on never so low a level, yet mother love is the holy thing which roots itself in the deepest soil of our nature, and holds us, even when only a memory, through the whole of a life of temptations. It abides because our heart knows that it is good, and because it stands every test. A book that has come through a holy human life when God moved the man, and which bears a living message to all who go to it for help and comfort, is safe in any sort of a crucible. We may as well be afraid of losing the sky—for the only way we can lose either is by losing our own power of perception.

The question whether the Bible is entirely composed of such æonian books is merely a question of fact, and cannot be settled by a theory. These books that now remain have come to us after many centuries of sifting, and many books of lower quality have dropped out because they could not pass the high test of spiritual worth. *These* will last so long as they continue to inspire those who go to them for a message and that will, we believe, be as long as men have a hunger for a knowledge of God and a perception of spiritual realities. All this is independent of the conclusions of scientific study. Such conclusions will no more affect the spiritual value of these divine messages than the new science of the universe has destroyed the unspeakable worth of Dante's Paradiso, which is fashioned on the old astronomy, or the new historical criticism which proves Macbeth a legend destroys the mighty moral meaning of Shakespeare's great poem. Everything turns on spiritual values, on intrinsic worth, on the quality of the message. A diamond is a diamond regardless of the fact that it can be analysed by the chemist and proved to be composed of carbon.

We find, then, that there are two elemental truths which furnish the ground and basis of a divine revelation to man : First, there is something in man to which God can speak, and secondly, a man's personality may become so spiritualized and sensitized that God can speak through him truths that lie above the level of ordinary men, and so the message proves a revelation—a master light—to help men's visions for all time. The sensitive plate photographs the star which the human eye fails to see, and so too the inspired man sees and declares what escapes the common eye. But its value lies in its power to make *us* see, and its authority is simply and solely the authority of truth, *i.e.* its power of producing conviction. It is never an authority which bans investigation and compels blind submission ; it is rather the authority which enforces itself solely by opening the eyes of the soul to see the truth—convincing vision. The inspiration is possible because God has found a man through whom He can speak, and the message becomes a revelation, because through it other men are able to see—or at the least to guess at—what the first man saw.

But after all, great as a book-revelation is, it is a clear fact that the centre around which the Christian centuries revolve is not a book, nor a group of books. It is not the words of holy men, moved by the spirit of God, which make our Christian religion a fact. The Christian religion centres around a Personality, who claims to reveal or manifest God as no book ever could. And unless we can find some ground for this supreme revelation—the Incarnation—we cannot hope to tell, in any intelligible way, what the basis of our religion is. Of course we do not propose to touch the old metaphysical problems of how two personalities—a human and divine—could exist in one person, nor whether He suffered as man or as God, nor whether He foresaw or did not foresee all things. None of that. Here is the fact—a single life which has revealed to us the nature of God and the nature of man, what God is, and what man may become. What it means is, of course, that God and man are not and never were foreign and unrelated. There is nothing in the nature of things human or divine to make an incarnation unexpected. There is something in every man God can speak to. There have been men through whom He could speak, because He could move them spiritually. We find at length one single Personality who was sinless, who lived entirely open to God, who had a sole purpose—to do His will, and from it this truth emerges that this Personality is a complete expression of Divinity and Humanity. It is no metaphysical puzzle, it is a concrete fact—the fact of facts—that One Life has expressed both God and man. The moment humanity is perfected and lifted, as here, to its supreme height, and no mark of the beast is on it, it can equally well call itself divinity, and the moment God shows Himself adequately to the world He does it in terms of humanity. Deity and humanity form no stubborn dualism. The two natures belong together, and in Christ they were together—not as two natures, but as one nature expressing both.

But the incarnation loses its meaning, if it does not bring with it—as it does—the mighty implication that a union of humanity and divinity is grounded in the very nature of man as a rational and spiritual being. There are all possible degrees of union, from the thin and slender thread which draws a prodigal home to the Father, up through the unselfish love of a saint, to the unparalled oneness of Father and Son which Christ has manifested in solitary completeness.

The incarnation was possible because divinity and humanity could be expressed in one life, and now that this fact is forever clear, because it is realised, the goal of our religion becomes a well-grounded hope, and a soundly-based purpose. The goal is nothing less than a union with God and the attainment of sonship with Him, or put in other words, the realization of complete spiritual well-being and well-doing, through correspondence with the divine will. The religious life—in so far as it is religious—is at once human and divine, and without the possibility of both aspects united in a single life no religion worthy of the name could be possible. This fact—the union of divine and human aspects in one person—prepares the way for the consideration of the basis and meaning of faith ? What is the criterion or authority of faith ? How do we know that the objects of faith are real, that the things which are not seen are eternal ? It must first of all be clearly understood that there is no schism, no opposition, between faith and reason. We do not use one as far as it will go and then take up the other. In fact, there is no knowledge apart from faith. Every truth, whether of common sense or of science, rests in the last resort upon some irreducible *conviction*, which is after all what we mean by faith.

It is not something different from reason ; it is, rather, reason working unconsciously. The moment one tries to analyse love, or to explain beauty, or to get an ultimate ground of duty, he is driven back to one of these irreducible convictions of the heart, which are not contrary to reason, which are essentially and implicitly rational, but which, nevertheless, cannot be dissected into lower terms and expressed in the coinage of thought. These ultimate realities are their own all-sufficient witness to our consciousness, and the certitude which the human spirit has in this immediate response of the heart to primary truths, is not weaker but stronger than reasoned knowledge ; and without such immediate response no knowledge would ever be possible.

Every man's act involves a primary faith and can be explained only on the assumption of an unproved conviction. But each successive act tests the worth of his faith and the validity of his convictions, until at length he completely forgets that he is in a world of unproved ultimates, and on his convictions he predicts eclipses and makes laws for the universe. Now religious faith is not something totally different from this—it is not belief in the testimony of some foreign authority— it is the immediate response of the soul to a spiritual fact, a divine truth, a living presence which it feels to be true, because it brings with it the unmistakeable witness and conviction of reality, just as beauty and love do. It would be impossible

to prove the freedom of the will of a man who
did not have this inward conviction of personal
freedom. No man would ever believe in God in
any real sense, if he did not find Him involved in
these primary convictions of his heart. It is
because the infinite and the finite, the divine and
the human, are in necessary relation to each other
that religious faith is ever possible, just as it is
because the world we see and the perceiving self
belong together that we have any basis for objective knowledge. The ear alone would never convince us of the existence of light, for the ear has
no relations with light. The eye does it, because it
has something in common with light. So it is that
the soul has an inner witness for spiritual realities,
and this inner witness is faith. The soul has no
criterion of certitude outside itself, for that would
involve a contradiction, as though the eye could
get some other eye to prove to it that it sees.

But this primary, irreducible conviction and
response of the inner spirit to a spiritual truth, is
capable of imperial expansion, for now the whole
meaning of life centres in its progress toward
spiritual reality. From the very nature of the case
faith is no mere passive, receptive state. It is the
soul's grasp of divine reality, and therefore it implies both vision and obedience to it. In a word,
it is dynamic—it is the movement of the whole
self toward the goal which it sees. It is the
ground of all spiritual activity, and each test of
truth, each experience of spiritual validity, each

victory of faith, increases the power of faith. It is, too, a characteristic of faith, that it wins and possesses its object, so that the object ceases to be a mere external goal. This throws light on Paul's conception of the spiritual Christ, who through faith—and Paul's faith is always dynamic—becomes an inner possession of the believer. As many as believe in Christ *put Him on. He becomes the life* through faith. The object of life is to *win Christ.* Such a faith is constructive, it means an ever higher spiritual life through apprehension of more spiritual reality, and spiritual perception becomes the achievement of a truer and larger personal life through faith.

Such a faith far from lessening the value and meaning of revelation, is the very ground on which a divine revelation becomes recognised as of value and can be wrought into spiritual character. The soul which has learned to recognise the Spirit's voice will not underprize what He has spoken through some higher, diviner soul ; on the contrary it will feel the power of inspiration as an artist feels the power and authority of an old master, who is on a level which he never hopes to reach. But inspiration could never be recognised as inspiration had not each soul the implicit capacity for it, and no words would ever be regarded as a revelation if the soul itself had not a first-hand sense of what revelation implies. It is in this way that faith becomes the *test* of things not seen, and the realities of conscience, love and faith become not less, but more sure to us than the things we touch and see with sense-organs. We trust

> " With faith that comes of self-control
> The truths that never can be proved,
> Until we close with all we loved
> And all we flow from, soul in soul."

When it is once clearly realised that faith is not the mere blind acceptance of what somebody else has seen, but rather the vision itself, we are ready to see what the communion and fellowship of the saints mean. Personal religion, on this basis, involves participation in the divine life. Keeping the faith is synonymous with keeping the life, *i.e.*, the vital connection with the divine Spirit. Two Christians are, therefore, not two bare atomic individuals who can live an unrelated life. They are rather like two branches of one vine, or two organs of one body. Their participation in the divine life, which we have found to be the primary fact of true religion, carries with it organic relation with each other. In a material system, held together by the force of gravitation like our solar system, the change of position of one body affects the whole system and makes every other body adjust itself. Much more so is this true in a spiritual system. The City of God, the Kingdom of Heaven, is a spiritual society in which each individual member makes his own independent contribution to sainthood, his own peculiar living stone to the growing Temple, yet he makes it not apart from but because he is taken up into the organic whole, and the fellowship and association and power of the body enable him to realise his life.

The church, then, is not a mere aggregation of individuals, not a composite of atomic elements. Such a church would be no more vital than a pile of cannon balls. It would stand only so long as some authoritative creed held it together. It would have no inward power of adjusting itself to a changing environment. There would be no ground of assurance that it would permanently abide. On the other hand, a church which is an organism rather than an organisation, which is formed not by aggregation of elements but by spiritual relationship and through union in a common divine centre whose power permeates the farthest circumference, has all the capacity for adjustment that life has. It makes its own bones and structure. It lives in its environments and partly changes the environment and partly yields to it. It progresses in the main because it has the life of God in it and its crises are like the crises in individual spiritual life —for the testing and perfecting of character. Like a growing man, its grasp and apprehension will change as it goes from one height of life to another and no conclusions of one age can have ¹ an arbitrary and eternal authority over other ages. The permanent authority is the central life, which will always be consistent with itself. " The anointing teacheth," that is, the Spirit abides to guide the church. Therefore church councils and ecclesiastical officials are not authoritative in the hierarchical sense. There is no man on the earth and no recorded ecclesiastical decision which a soul is bound to obey in its spiritual attitude or in its relations with God. As each soul must go alone into the unknown when death comes, so each soul must settle its own relations with God, and it must be free from restraint to work out its salvation, as it apprehends God's will.

But *if* believers are organic, are members one of another, then the life and character of one individual must be largely shaped by the body, and the personal life must be determined by the spiritual society of which it is a part. In a true sense the Church is authoritative, as we have already found the Scriptures authoritative. It is, however, not an authority of compulsion, but the authority of inspiration. It is the authority of conviction, and there is no spiritual value in any other. It is an authority which makes its way, not by forcing assent, but by winning it through an appeal to that which is "likest God within the soul." Every attainment in religion is the result, not of submission to some outward law or external authority, but of obedience to a law which has become the very essence and principle of our own being. The Kingdom of Heaven, the City of God, the fellowship of saints, is the corporate life of such autonomous selves, participating in the divine life and in the lives of each other, so that every individual is more than an individual !

The basis of religion is, therefore, to be sought

in the primary fact that God Himself is love—a self-revealing and self-giving Being, and that man, by the very constitution of his being, is capable of receiving Him, of responding to Him, of uniting with Him and of being taken up into the divine life. The soul no more needs a proof of His love and His presence than the eye does of the existence of the sunlight which it sees. Deep calls unto deep ; the deep in God calls to the deep in man, and they know each other. It is because the divine thought can be put into human terms and the human life can be wrought into the divine likeness, that inspiration and revelation have been possible or that they have a meaning for us. It is because of this mighty fact that an Incarnation could be made which possesses an eternal value for man, and presents the goal of creation. The meaning of church authority and of historic truth is rooted in the same fact. The manifestation of the divine Spirit in history, and in the organisation of spiritual men speaks with peculiar power to the soul which is itself in immediate relationship with the same Spirit. One more conclusion forces itself, namely, that religion is to be a permanent feature of life—that man is " incurably religious." In an unfolding, developing thing one may never with absolute certainty predict what characteristics may appear in some remote future, but we may safely believe that, if what we call religion, in some future period drops out of the race, it will be only because some diviner thing, which we cannot possibly foresee, has taken its place. The relation between God and man, which is the ground of religion, is involved in the nature of both, and it is difficult to see how it can ever go while God is God and man is man. " We need not fear that we can lose anything by the progress of the soul. The soul may be trusted to the end. That which is so beautiful and attractive as these relations, must be succeeded and supplanted only by what is more beautiful, and so on for ever." *

* Emerson's Essay on "Love."

SOURCES OF QUAKERISM IN THE
SCRIPTURES.

II.

SOURCES OF QUAKERISM IN THE SCRIPTURES.

THOSE who are familiar with the Journal of George Fox are aware that he does not represent himself as arriving at the truths which he proclaimed, by a study of the Scriptures. He tells us in regard to the ideas which seemed to many of his generation " *dangerously new*," that they were "opened to him." He nowhere tells us that he came upon the fundamental principles which constitute his contribution to religious thought, through the interpretation of Scripture passages.

And yet the moment he began to defend his position against the priests of his day, he appealed to Scripture, precisely as Paul did, though the latter also distinctly declared that his gospel was a personal revelation to him. And in this appeal to Scripture, Fox at once made clear the significant fact that he knew the Bible as probably no other man in England at the time did. In fact, his mind was saturated with it, so saturated that truths were deposited in him from it like a silent dew, without his realising whence they came. To the end of his life he never knew how much he owed to the Book, which had become a part of the structure of his thought; just as we never realise how much the atmosphere is to us while our lungs are always full of it.

Therefore in speaking of the sources or roots of Quakerism in the Bible we do not mean to imply that Fox or the early Friends explicitly thought out their principles from biblical texts, or that they saw precisely the same relation between their views and Scripture passages as we shall find when we look at the two side by side. Nor do we mean to imply that there was no immediate working of the revealing Spirit directly to them. On the contrary, we are sure there was such immediate working, but we also think that many truths which were implicit and unexpanded in Scripture became the possessions of their minds by a subconscious process, somewhat as a spring breaks out in a man's field after a subterranean passage from another source.

Be this as it may, we wish at any rate to speak in this paper of some of the Scripture passages, particularly in the New Testament, which are the implicit sources of Quakerism.

We shall select one single passage from the Old Testament which so far as we remember was never definitely quoted by Fox, but which expresses what he was all his life saying, though sometimes none too clearly in his phraseology, " In Thy light shall

we see light." (Psalm xxxvi. 9.) It is a simple
way of saying that nothing can be understood out
of relation to God, that nothing is clear until it is
viewed in its relation to Him. It means too that
the world is full of light only so far as it is full of
God, and that therefore He is the master light of
all our seeing. Even the Bible itself would have
no spiritual meaning for us were there not something in us which perceived and apprehended the
truth there expressed, and *that something* which
perceives divine truth is itself of divine origin.
That is, the light by which we see God and
spiritual things is a light which comes from God,
just as the light by which we see the star comes
from the star. In God's light we see light. Fox
calls this the light within (and we shall speak more
in detail of it in a later chapter), but he never
means that it is a light which a human soul has
apart from God, but always the light which the
soul has from its relation to God, *i.e.* we see light
in His light.

In the synoptic gospels, the most significant
passage for our present purpose is found in the
words of Jesus known as "Beatitudes": "The
pure in heart see God." As the only obstacle to
vision of God is impurity of heart, necessarily the
business of life can never be to "tithe mint and
anise," to play at religion, but to cleanse the heart.
It becomes a man's sole and single task "To make
his heart a stainless mirror for his God." These
words of the Master carry us directly away from a

religion of externals to a religion which is inward
and vital, and which deals at once with life and
character.   No amount of psalm singing, or church-
going, no amount of creed-signing, or pious atti-
tudes, could make a man see God, if his heart was
still impure and if he was still clinging to some
pet sin ; and this fact was as clear as daylight to
George Fox, who himself went straight to the
heart of things and based his whole message on
this practical truth, that there can be no substitute
in religion for purity of heart.

This fundamental ground, viz., that religion
begins with a more or less clear vision of God,
and that the vision depends solely on purity of
heart, is reason enough, were there no others, why
the rituals and ordinances of the historic church
are discarded by Friends. The man who hates
sham and hypocrisy with all the earnestness of his
moral nature cannot brook any religious cloak
which can be put on and taken off for occasions ;
he will have nothing which stops short of the
soul's vision.   The religious teacher must be a
spiritual oculist whose business is not to furnish
light, but to tell men how to remove their catar-
acts and to adjust their sight ; for, behold, God is
always visible the moment the inward eye is clear !

Origen used to say that nobody could fully understand the profound spiritual truths of John's
Gospel who had not, like its author, lain on the
breast of Jesus.   This Gospel is an interpretation
of Christianity by one who has grasped its inner

meaning rather than a synoptic sketch of the life of Jesus, and for this reason it can be appreciated and appropriated only by those who possess spiritual penetration. It undoubtedly had more direct influence in shaping the thought and bent of the early Friends than any other single book, either within or outside the Bible, though even here the influence is perhaps more subconscious than distinctly realised. John regards Christ as a manifestation of God and through this manifestation it becomes revealed that God is not a foreign Being, living in splendid isolation apart from the world, but the ground and substance of all things that *are*. He is a *spirit*, and so limited to no place. He is *light* and so from His nature pervasive and illuminative, destroying darkness and evil by showing Himself. He is *truth*, and so can be relied upon as real and undeviating. In other words, He is, supremely, character and not a blind fate. He is *love* and so He gives Himself to men. The incarnation is no afterthought, no scheme, no sudden miracle. It is the natural expression of the essential being of God. He is love, and so He must show Himself redemptive. It is thus that the early Friends think of God and it is thus that they interpret Him. The Calvinistic idea of sovereignty is lost in this Johannine conception of a loving Father who shares His life and light and truth with us and whose dwelling place is no more in the heavens than it is in the Shekinah within a spiritual man.

It is for this reason that worship takes on a wholly new signification, *i.e.*, new as compared with the conception of it in the churches of the time. Friends came together not to please God or to flatter Him, or to call Him down or to lecture about Him. They came together to meet *with Him* and to enjoy Him. It was not necessary to *do* anything to bring Him any more than it is to bring the sunlight in the morning. The only human action needed, they felt, was to open the soul's windows. If anybody failed to find Him, the trouble was within. The fact remained that where any met in Christ's name, *i.e.*, with that openness of heart and singleness of will which Christ illustrated, the divine presence would be felt, and every human cup held out would be filled to the brim.

/ The organic character of the Christian life which John frequently emphasises was also a prominent feature of early Quakerism. If John never thinks of God as isolated, apart, alone ; no more does he ever think of man, or at least a spiritual man, as isolated or out of organic relation. In fact, such a conception is essentially irrational and impossible. Life involves organic relation. Who could be a spiritual being if he were insulated from God, any more than he could live in the exhausted receiver of an air pump ? The spiritual life advances precisely in proportion as the soul unites with its source of life and becomes vital by such union— branch with vine. But such union involves further

organic relations with one's brethren. So long as one persists in guarding his own self-centred isolation and refuses to lose his life in outreaching love and sympathy and sacrifice, he does not find his life in God. A member which will not co-ordinate with the other members of the body, but asserts its independence, loses at length its organic union altogether, and its connection with the head becomes paralyzed. Significant indeed are the words : "That they may be one in us, as thou Father art in me and I in thee." It is out of this ground that the Society of Friends springs into existence. It is in its first conception not an organization but an organism. The members live and act primarily through their relation with Christ, thus they all become organic branches in one common vine-stock. No member can be a spiritual creature and live his independent life. He has lost his isolated life to find his organic life with his brethren. We shall see in a later chapter how this principle affects every phase of the Quaker's outward life and how it makes him a practical reformer and missionary ; but for the moment we are concerned with stating that the ideal which takes shape in Christ's prayer and in John xv. is literally accepted by the Quaker as the basis of his relation to God and his relation to men.

John presents a type of salvation which is present, not future alone. He finds no necessity for postponing blessedness and joy. "He that believeth on the Son *hath* everlasting life." " He that hath the Son *hath* life." " He *is passed* from death unto life." " This *is* eternal life." " We *are* in Him." " This *is* the victory that overcometh the world, even your faith." There is no breach between this life and the other—no chasm. The only chasm is between the self-life of sin and the life in Christ. When that chasm has been passed there are no other necessary breaks, for death is only an episode, the bursting of the bud for the full flower to appear. There is no dualism of earth and heaven. The only dualisms here are light and darkness, love and selfishness, sin and eternal life. "Verily, verily, the hour cometh, in fact *now is* when the dead shall hear the voice of the Son of God and they that hear shall live." (John v. 25.)

This present type of salvation, of eternal life, as a realised and conscious fact is everywhere a characteristic of early Quakerism. Fox does not stake his hope of heaven on written promises, but he claims a spiritual experience which is to him an all-sufficient earnest of eternal blessedness. He can say with the same assurance as John can : "We know that we have passed from death unto life," *i.e.*, the last and only chasm has been closed. We shall see later what an effect this conception of a present salvation had upon the early Friends.

No intelligent, robust Christian ever lived who laid less stress and emphasis on the externals in religion, or who had a profounder grasp of the spiritual and essential ground of religion than the

Apostle Paul. Hear him : " I did not receive this
gospel from man." " It came to me through revelation of Jesus Christ." " God shined into my
heart to give knowledge." " It pleased God to
reveal his Son in me." " Man's wisdom," " the
wisdom of the world," is of no avail in the search
for spiritual truth. " Divine things are spiritually
discerned." " If we have known Christ after the
flesh, we will know Him so no more." " We have
the mind of Christ." These are some of the well-
known passages of Paul, which if taken by themselves as a complete expression of Christianity
would land one in the most extreme mysticism
and antinomianism. It is needless to say that in
spite of these extreme expressions, Paul never even
approached a dangerous individualism and that his
apparent mysticism was in perfect balance with his
clear and open sight of practical truth and with an
organic solidarity of believers in Christ. If his
head was above, his feet were solidly on the earth.

He makes use at every point of his vast fund of
acquired experiences. Everything which his life
has furnished him is drawn upon to express and
illustrate the things of the Spirit. His culture, and
grace, and versatility, his shrewdness in grasping a
situation, his skill and deftness, are as prominent as
his mysticism. He saw what was essential in order
to establish and make permanent the church, as
clearly as he saw his personal heavenly vision.

It is, nevertheless, impossible to ignore the sub-
jective and mystical element in Paul, and it surely

had its influence on George Fox, and, in a less degree, on the other primitive Friends. Both Paul and Fox call their new birth a divine *fiat lux.* " It pleased God who caused light to shine out of darkness to shine into my heart to give the light of the knowledge of the glory of God in the face of Jesus Christ." So wrote the Apostle. " When all my hopes in all men were gone so that I had nothing outwardly to help me . . . then, Oh, then, I heard a voice which said, 'There is one, even Jesus Christ, who can speak to thy condition.'" So spoke the Quaker. The Pauline view that spiritual things are spiritually discerned by such as have the mind of Christ is essentially the Quaker view, and this principle underlies (as we shall see) the Quaker conception of ministry, and for that matter all gifts for spiritual service.

Paul further teaches that the individual Christian must personally experience in his own life the redemptive work and process of Christ. He does not simply look upon the life of Christ as an historic fact which brings salvation by a mere act of belief. It is a mighty divine process, writ large in Jesus Christ, to be realised and recapitulated in each one of us. The life, and death and resurrection of Christ reveal the law of spiritual life by which we are all to live and the victory over sin and death becomes ours through participation in His life and in His Spirit.

In fact participation in Christ, and so in the divine life, is fundamental in Paul's conception of salvation. Faith with Him is never an intellectual belief or assent. It is always a vital or dynamic process of appropriating Christ Himself. "The life I now live in the flesh I live by the faith of the Son of God." "That Christ may dwell in your hearts by faith." "Put on Christ." "That I may win Christ." "That I may know Him and the power of His resurrection." This view at once removes religion from the realm of theory and abstract metaphysics and makes it personal and experimental. It aims not to prove the truth of some technical doctrine but to realise as a glorious fact that "Christ is formed in you." This living union of the believer with Christ who progressively becomes one's life is a central feature of Paul's teaching, and it is a cornerstone of Quakerism. We are here no longer in the realm of anatomy, but of biology. We are dealing with life and not with skeletons articulated with wire. Every feature of such a religion is vital and practical, and bears directly upon the production of a spiritual life which is capable of unlimited future expansion.

This Pauline view of Christ as the believer's life involves a most important conclusion which he himself drew with emphasis. It means that all Christians are organic as members of a body. He even goes so far as to express a belief in the unity and spirituality of the whole universe, which moves toward the realisation of one divine event— the unveiling of the sons of God. Individualism and isolated personality are impossible in such a

spiritual kingd..m. Each individual realises his life
through his relationships. He dies unto himself
that he may live unto the larger divine life. God
is thought of no longer as foreign and dual to us,
but we live in Him and He in us, as far as we
truly live, and the whole spiritual life is a living
unto God. This participation of the believer in an
organic spiritual whole, so that each is a living
stone in a spiritual temple, indwelt and vitalized by
the Holy Spirit; so that, to use another figure,
each is an articulated member in a living body,
each functioning with all and receiving its life and
power from its Head, is a fundamental view of
early Quakerism and one which cannot be lost
without endangering the whole system of our faith.

We shall consider but two more points of contact, though it will occur to everybody that many
of our omissions are as important as our so-called
contacts. We are dealing, however, it must be
remembered, not with testimonies or with super-
ficial features, but with elements involved in the
very inward structure of Quakerism.

In the Apocalypse, the glorified Christ is seen as
the one "who hath loved us and washed us from
our sins in His own blood and hath made us kings
and priests unto God." (I use the authorized
version which George Fox himself read.) A similar
expression is found in 1 Peter, describing the
believers in Christ as "a royal priesthood." Both
passages carry us back, in association and connection, to the great words at Caesarea Philippi : "I

give unto thee the keys of the kingdom of heaven."

These expressions present a conception of the Christian life which demands a much profounder examination than it has usually received. Let us see what it means : A person who has felt the significance of the divine love and who has been washed from his sins—or, to put it in terms of the gospel account, a person who has had an inward revelation of Jesus as the Christ, the Son of God—becomes through his transformed nature and spiritual character a centre of spiritual power, and just in so far as his personal faith gives him spiritual insight he possesses authority, *i.e.*, he is a key-bearer in the kingdom. When Dante stands purged of the last mark of his sin he hears a voice which says : " Thee o'er thyself I crown and mitre." The soul has come at last where it knows good and evil and prefers the good. It has served under the law, it has made choice of sonship, and that involves the freedom and royalty of the sons of God. Each person of this sort is a nucleus of a church and a propagator of the Gospel to others. There is no place for a priestly class or for that matter for any kind of a class, for all are priests. We level up instead of leveling down. There will be all degrees of abilities and of gifts, for authority and efficiency are determined by capacity and personality, but every individual is, to the limit of his spiritual range, a king and a priest. This principle permits no official hierarchy, no church authority which invades by right of position the domain of the individual. In fact it annihilates priestcraft and official tyranny in the church and establishes the priesthood of believers. But this does not mean that each individual is a law unto himself and that he may run unhindered into the vagaries of his own sweet will even to the anarchy of the church. Believers in Christ, as we have seen, constitute an organism—it is a body of royal priests—and one member, though authoritative in his sphere, can no more be allowed to rule or wreck the whole than one finger joint should be allowed to direct and control the whole body. Such a joint would need amputation, and such a member has ceased to be organic. This priesthood of believers—with a spiritual authority in each proportionate to his natural gifts and his appropriation of power through union with Christ—is again an essential feature of Quakerism. It underlies the conception of membership, the idea of ministry and the method of conducting the business of the church. It crowns and mitres every Christian who has a living personal faith and it leaves every soul free to attain to any height of experience which is within his range. It avoids at the same time a tyranny and an anarchy. Its authority is the authority which the master who knows has over the pupil who wants to know, and the obedience which it receives is the obedience which the learner who wants to know gives to the teacher who knows. As the royal-priesthood conception gives no ground for tyranny, so too it

gives no ground for fossilization. It has power
to loose or bind. Its historic positions have no
sacred quality—no sacramental virtue. Like any
other body it lives in its environment and conforms
to it. This is most certainly the New Testament
conception of the church, and it is a germ principle
in early Quakerism.

We have already indicated the practical character
of New Testament Christianity and we find the
same mark upon this seventeenth century interpretation of it which we are studying. Paul's test of a
Christian is whether he "walks after the Spirit";
John's test is whether he "walks in the light."
They both mean the same thing. To neither
apostle is it enough for a person to possess a
satisfactory theology, or to claim an exalted spiritual experience. Neither of them deals for a
moment with abstractions. Truth is not something
merely to be *held*, but something to be *expressed* in life,
in personality, in deed. It is easy for some minds to
construct theology and it is a short step to the
conclusion that a system of theology is a good in
itself and a sufficient indication of lofty attainment.
It is easy also to claim spiritual guidance, an
infallible inner light, a complete possession by the
Holy Spirit. But both theology and claim to
guidance are here subjected to a practical test. In
the last resort a man's religion is determined by
his "walk," which includes his whole life-attitude.
He may have a system of beliefs adjusted in
perfect order and buttressed by logic and countless

scripture passages and yet he is "nothing," he is
"clanging brass" without a positive, *practical love*
which expresses itself through his life and gives
convincing evidence that he is joined to the Lord
in one spirit. He may claim that he has no will
of his own and that all his impulses are sur-
rendered to the Spirit who speaks and works
through him, but Paul's first question will be, Does
he walk according to that Spirit, *i.e.*, does his life
authenticate his claim? Does his life carry irresis-
tibly the conviction that the Spirit of the infinite
God of love and righteousness and truth is speaking and working through him? He may easily
say that he has an inner light which illumines him
and which directs his steps, but John's question
will be, Does he walk in the light, *i.e.*, do his
words and actions indicate that he is the recipient
of light from a heavenly source? and is his life a
source of light and guidance to others? These
practical tests of the two apostles find expression
in many passages in every part of the New
Testament. In fact it can be safely said that no
New Testament writer knows anything of a religion
of theory, a religion of profession or a religion
which is summed up in theological doctrine.

We find this same situation everywhere manifest
in early Quakerism. It was never a mere theory
or doctrine ; it was a method or manner of life.
If it began in an immediate sense of relationship
to God and of illumination from Him, it reached
through and ramified and transformed every rela-

tion and act of life however ordinary and common. The Quaker's whole life flowed out from and illustrated the fundamental truth of his faith. He could call no voice divine which did not conform to the highest moral conduct ; he could heed no revelation which did not tend to elevate and purify the life. He could profess nothing which was not grounded in reality. His life must be as his teaching : "brave, pure, truthful, beneficent, hopeful and cheerful." Fox never deviated from this consistency of life with truth. He says that the Lord opened to him, that here was a principle by which all might be reformed—the priests might be reformed, the lawyers might be reformed, the physicians might be reformed, namely, "as all believe in the light, and walk in the light," and so "become children of the light and of the day of Christ," "the spiritual heavenly man." ("Fox's Journal," *p. 70.*)

MYSTICISM AND THE MYSTICS.

III.

MYSTICISM AND THE MYSTICS.

RELIGIOUS mysticism is an attempt to realise the presence of God in the soul. It is grounded on the fact that a direct intercourse between the human soul and God is possible ; and its ultimate goal is the attainment of a state in which God shall cease to be an external object and shall become known by an experience of the heart. The mystic refuses to be satisfied with any substitute *for* God, or to stop with any "third thing" between the soul and God, be that so-called "third thing" never so exalted a representative of Him or means of showing Him forth.

His aim is not to know about God, but to know *Him*. He cannot be satisfied even with what God has said or done in the past, for his consuming purpose is to have God himself. He rejoices in God's promises, but he sets a higher value still on his personal acquaintance with God and His character, so that he needs no longer to ask what the Father has promised, since now he knows what He Himself *is*, and he trusts Him even where He has not promised. Mysticism has always been a protest against formalism and authority ; and it has always, when healthy, emphasised inspiration, spirituality and personality. Whenever Christianity has crystallised into an unvital system, either of authority or creed, and has proved in this form inadequate to feed or expand the souls of men, the mystic has come to proclaim a direct and living way to God and to announce communion with God as a fact of experience. Whenever the church has satisfied itself with performing the functions of a vicar to the distant, absentee God, dispensing grace through its few sacred channels, while leaving the human heart still hungry for its proper food, the mystic has come to declare the *nearness* of God, the possibility of a certainty of Him through immediate contact and the soul's sure privilege of rejoicing in Him.

There are innumerable types of mysticism and all possible degrees of it—some rising into the clear light of vision and some giving indications of a shockingly diseased personality or a sadly morbid condition. I shall only outline its spiritual message, illustrating it through some of its best exponents, and content myself with pointing out some of its errors and dangerous tendencies.

We will consider first what seems to me the most important aspects of religious mysticism, and which I have made central in my definition, *viz* : its attempt to realise the presence of God in the

soul. If such an experience *is possible*, we are
dealing with one of the most significant facts which
a human being can ever be concerned with ; and
if it is *not* possible, religious truth must always be
something more or less foreign to our experience
and something which rests solely on external
authority. The question of such possibility, then,
becomes supremely important. There can be no
doubt, in the mind of anyone who has studied
Paul's letters, that he claimed not only that it is
possible to realise the divine presence in the soul,
but that he himself did realise it. Religion for
him meant a divine life wrought within ; it was
not the acceptance of a certain system of things,
or a belief in transactions—or at least not primarly
that ; it was a consciousness within himself that
everything had become new and of God. The
natural in him was raised to the spiritual by a
union with the divine, and the spiritual became in
a very real sense natural. Christianity was for him,
what Edward Caird has said it *should* be, " a process
by which the natural man in whom the life of
Christ is an external fact is converted into the
spiritual man to whom the belief in Christ is one
with the consciousness of Himself." " Christ liveth
in me." "For me to live is Christ." "He that is
joined to the Lord is one spirit." "Filled with all
the fulness of God." These are a few of the
words which express the idea which we mean.
It was with him not an attainment through ecstacy
or by a supernatural irruption into the domain of

his personality, it was the normal result of co-operation with God. He perceived that God wanted his life and he also perceived that he needed God to complete his own life. God reached after him, and he reached up in co-operation. Their natures met in his personality; his being became spiritualised and God worked through him. The process went on until his life became "hid with Christ in God" and he could no longer tell where the circle of his own human personality stopped and where the divine began, as one cannot draw the exact line where ocean and river meet.

The Neo-Platonic Mystics, as they are sometimes called from the influence upon them of Platonic philosophy, generally believe in the possibility of a union with God, but such attainment is rare and laborious. God and the soul have no natural affinity for each other, as with Paul. They do not of right belong together and find their true life in each other. For Plotinus, the father of this school of mystics, himself not a Christian, the chasm between God and man is wide and unspanned. It must be scaled if at all by desperate climbing, and the divine glory breaks only when the last vestige of "the creature" has been removed. The "union" is attained by an ecstacy and when the soul returns to itself it brings back nothing with it which can be used in this undivine world. So with all mystics of the speculative, Neo-Platonic class, the soul's attain-

ment of joy and calm in God is reached by
mystical ladders of purgation, prayer, contemplation, illumination, toward the goal of union. Each
mystic has a different ladder or ascent, but they
all climb up to reach and merge themselves into a
far-off God who is unknowable except through
union wherein "like knows like."

The German mystics of the Fourteenth Century
bring the emphasis back to the original Pauline
position, that God is near, yes, immanent, and that
we live and move and have our being in Him.
The great figures of this group are Eckhart, John
Tauler, Ruysbrock, Suso, and the unknown author
of *Theologica Germanica*. Eckhart, born *circa* 1251,
taught that every soul, even in the simplest believer as well as in the greatest pope, has a
"*fünklein*" or divine "spark" which is at the
apex of our being and forms its essence—an uncreated essence. It is the ground of eternal nature,
the reason for the soul's longing for God. It is
the "divine soul centre," the shekinah, the original
part of the soul which "drew from out the bound-
less deep." This inner "spark" is divine—it is
God, but it becomes our life only as we make it
ours. It is the business of life to bring the outer
completely under the control of this inner centre
of force, *i.e.*, to vitalise and spiritualise the whole
man from within out—what Paul calls letting God
work in us to will and to do. This victory, this
attainment, Eckhart says, comes not without
struggle and battle. Spiritual life is not a calm

innocence—it is the fruit of strife and struggle.
"That a man has a peaceful and restful life in
God is good; that a man endures a painful life
with patience is better, but that a man has his
rest in the midst of a painful life is best." "When
the man's will becomes God's will it is good; but
when God's will becomes man's will, that is better."
Again he cries out: "Thou shall sink thy thine-
ness, and thy thine shall become a Mine in His
Mine." Only God can properly say "I am," and
human personality becomes a fact only when the
Eternal ground-form of being is realised in us.
Both Eckhart and Tauler call this, "God begetting
His Son in us." Thus we enter "His everlasting
Now." In this divine process God becomes man
and man becomes divine, *i.e.*, by grace man may
become what Christ eternally *is* by His very
nature.

John Tauler was one of the greatest practical
teachers and preachers and one of the bravest
souls of the pre-Reformation period. He, too, holds
that every man in the depth of his soul—the in-
most centre of himself—touches God. Hear him:
"God pours Himself into our spirits as the sun
rays forth its natural light into the air, and fills it
with sunshine; so that no eye can tell the difference between the sunshine and the air. If the
union of the sun and air cannot be distinguished,
how far less this divine union of the created and
the uncreated spirit." Our spirit is received and
swallowed up in the abyss which is its source!

Jacob Boehme of Gorlitz (born 1575) finds the same God in his heart that he finds in nature and he believes that the whole mystery of nature may be solved and read off by knowledge of and union with the God who manifests Himself within and who is always and everywhere like Himself.

These men proclaim as a fact that the vision, the glory, the aim, the ideal which make life great are not from us and do not rise within what is ordinarily called ourselves ; they break in upon us, but they claim that the attainment of life is reached only when our personality is no longer outside the circle of His being but has its life in Him, as a physical man lives in the air. We know of no clearer statement of this idea than the one found in the *Journal* of Amiel (p. 98, Vol. I.) :

"The centre of life is neither in thought nor in feeling, nor in will, nor even in consciousness so far as it thinks, feels, or wishes. For moral truth may have been penetrated and possessed in all these ways, and escape us still. Deeper even than consciousness there is our being itself, our very substance, our nature. Only those truths which have entered into this last region, which have become ourselves, become *spontaneous*, and involuntary, instinctive and unconscious are really our life —that is to say, something more than our property. So long as we are able to distinguish any space whatever between the truth and us, we remain outside it. The thought, the feeling, the desire, the consciousness of life, are not yet quite life.

But peace and repose can nowhere be found except in life and in eternal life, and the eternal life is the divine life—is God. To become divine is then the aim of life; then only can truth be said to be ours beyond the possibility of loss, because it is no longer outside us, nor even in us, but we are it and it is we; we ourselves are a truth, a will, a work of God."

We know to-day much more clearly than when these words were written that the self of which we are conscious is but a fraction of our real self. Most of the operations and activities of our life go on beneath the threshold of consciousness. Our conscious life of the moment is but a bubble heaved up from the subterranean life below. We are never absolutely sure of anything until we know it and do it subconsciously, as the musician's fingers know the keys and as the gymnast's feet know the tight-rope. It is this under life which determines all we do and how we do it. Whether a man is a genius or a fogy is largely a question of whether he has a rich and fertile subliminal life so near the surface that it supplies him on demand with what he wants for the occasion or not. No one was ever an artist, a poet, or an orator without that. No one can ever be wholly and dependably good until he is good beyond the knowing it, *i.e.*, until his subconscious self sets toward righteousness, as the ocean obeys the law of gravitation without knowing it. This is what Aristotle calls a moral dexterity of the soul.

Speaking religiously, it is what Paul calls being
"hid with Christ in God." Von Hartman defines
mysticism as a genius or aptitude for God through
the unconscious. The prophet, the saint, the
mystic, has a subliminal self that opens more
immediately upon the divine than others have, or
at least he is more sensitive to it, and therefore
he sees, as William Watson says :

> " Those master moments grow less rare,
> And oftener feels that nameless air
> Come rumoring from we know not where ;
> And touch at whiles
> Fantastic shores, the fringes fair
> Of fairy isles :
> And hails the mystic bird that brings
> News from the inner court of things,
> The eternal courier dove whose wings
> Are never furled :
> And hears the bubbling of the springs
> That feed the world."

We believe that every man's subliminal self *opens*
Godward, as the inlet opens to the sea, but the
mystics are they who have found it out as a fact
because the surges of the eternal Self broke upon
the shores of their personal being, and they have
realised that only sin could separate man and God.
This fundamental fact of mysticism, namely, the
immediate communion between the soul and God
and the possible realisation of the divine life, gives
a peculiar meaning to faith. Faith to the mystics
is not the adoption of a system of doctrine, but
much more, the soul's immediate perception of

truth—it is spiritual vision. It is *the condition* of spiritual life as eating is of physical life. It is not an intellectual, or an emotional state—it is rather *an act* of the whole personality. It precedes knowledge and is the ground of knowledge—"he that willeth shall know"; "he that believeth hath the witness." It gives reality to what the soul hungers and hopes for, and it becomes "the *test* of things not seen" with the physical eye. It is what Paul calls "the demonstration of the spirit." That means the soul's direct perception of a spiritual work going on within it, as little to be doubted as the beauty the artist sees or the harmony the musician hears. St. Teresa gives a good illustration of what we mean. When her "superiors" were trying to persuade her that her experiences were delusions, she answered : "If they who said this told me that a person who had just finished speaking to me, whom I knew well, was *not* that person, but they knew I fancied it, doubtless I should believe them, rather than what I had seen ; but if this person left behind him some jewels as pledges of his great love, and I found myself rich, having been poor, I could not believe them if I wished. And these jewels I could show them. For all who knew me saw clearly that my soul was changed ; the difference was great and palpable." Faith thus begins with the resolution to trust unfalteringly to what it feels to be true and ends with an experience which transcends ordinary knowledge in certainty. This is "the faith that

comes of self-control"—that rises in power and
surety with each test of experience. It is this,
too, that makes Wordsworth cry out : " Thanks to
the human *heart* by which we live." It is this
that grounds Paul's life forever in certainty : " I
know in whom I have believed." Therefore the
supreme attainment is the perfection of this truth
seeing faculty without which, in some degree,
spiritual religion would be impossible. The my-
steries of life are understood by living through
them.

The mystic, again, is profoundly aware of
spiritual laws. He knows that there is nothing
arbitrary, or capricious, or unethical in God's
world. He realises that it is as impossible to get
character,—or heaven either, without going through
the processes and experiences which win it, as it
is to move a load without a motive force. There
is for him no short cuts to any kind of glory
and no palm without an honest struggle. The
connection between holiness and blessedness is
as unvarying as between cause and effect. It is
beautifully illustrated in the " Paradiso" of that
great mediæval mystic, Dante. The poet is won-
dering how he has gone from earth to heaven
directly against the law of gravitation. His
heavenly guide answers that it is necessary for
free spirits to go up.

" Thou should'st not wonder more, if well I judge,
  At thine ascent, than at a rivulet
  From some high mount *descending* to the plains.

Marvel it would be in thee, if deprived
Of hindrance, thou wert seated down below,
As if on earth the living fire were quiet."
                              Paradiso C. I. 135-141.

It remains to be said that mystics are peculiarly
fond of symbols. A recent French writer, Récéjac,
says that "mysticism is an attempt to approach the
Absolute morally, and by means of symbols."
While an English writer, Nettleship, says that
"true mysticism is the belief that everything in
being what it is, is symbolic of something more."
Another English writer, Inge, says, "Every truth
we know is but the husk of a deeper truth."
There is a famous saying of old Hermes Trismeg-
istus, that "everything that is, is double." All his
life Goethe was proclaiming the fact that all things
transitory are symbolic and but garments of the
eternal spirit. Carlyle is the English, and Emerson
the American prophet of this truth. In high
spiritual moments Paul was clairvoyant, in the
lofty sense, and realised that the things seen are
temporal, while the things not seen, except *through*
these temporal things, are eternal. In such a
moment the author of Hebrews saw that the
things that are seen are not made of things which
do appear. It is because nature is symbolic that
Christ can say "Consider the lilies," and it em-
boldens Tennyson to say of "the flower in the
crannied wall,"

> "If I could understand
> What you are, root and all, and all in all,
> I should know what God and man is."

There is a prevalent belief that mystics are
dreamers, or at the best only seers of visions—not
active workers and doers of deeds. The belief is
partly true and partly false. It has been one of the
grave dangers of the mystic that he contents himself with "dreamily passive emotions" and makes
his highest good in life the attainment of "a
deedlessly passive and unspeakable rapture in God."
But an excessive quietist mood is a mark of
degenerate and not of true and healthy mysticism.
The great mystics who must be our types have
learned that every new truth, every new vision,
involves a new duty and leads to activity. It is
what Paul calls "obedience to the heavenly vision,"
and without which new heavenly visions would
surely not come.

In commenting on Mary and Martha as types of
contemplation and activity, Eckhart says : "Mary
hath *chosen* the good part ; that is, she is striving
to be as holy as her sister. Mary is still at school.
Martha has learnt her lesson. It is better to feed
the hungry than to see such visions as Paul saw."
Tauler says with beautiful simplicity : "If I were
not a priest, I should esteem it a gift of the Holy
Ghost that I was able to make shoes." "Works of
love are more acceptable to God," again he says,
"than lofty contemplation." Best of all, however,
are Tauler's words which embody a profound
spiritual law : "Never trust in a virtue that has not
been put into practice." The mystics who really
face the issues of life and who see that all spiritual

6

attainments are part of a divine process and not capricious gifts to a favoured few, all teach us that God's highest truth is given to those who make the best use of it. The healthy mystic is the one who *sees* and *does* and who learns to see more because he used what he found. Eckhart's plan is a safe one : "Take the nearest way Godwards, but be always sure to keep in motion on that way, until God's rest comes of itself."

There is a graver mistake than that of the passive or quietistic tendency, and one which many, if not most, mystics have made. They have divided man into a dualism and rejected a necessary half of him. They have said, and it is a mischievous doctrine, that the spiritual eye can see only when the eye of sense is closed. They have held that God can enter with His light only when the natural light of reason has been brought to naught. One of George Chapman's characters puts this idea well :

> " I'll build all inward—not a light shall ope
> The common outway—
> I'll therefore live in dark ; and all my light
> Like ancient temples let in at my top."

Coleridge means the same thing in his " Ode to Dejection : "

> " It were a vain endeavour
> Though I should gaze forever
> On that green light that lingers in the west,
> I may not hope from outward forms to win
> The passion and the life whose fountains are within."

That man is certainly on the wrong track who, when he starts out in a search for truth begins by destroying the very faculties which have been given to him for finding it and testing it. There are not two kinds of truth—that which our human faculties can discover, and that which lies beyond them. The divine does not begin where the human leaves off. If what we have been saying is true, the divine and the human belong together—in fact, without this, there is no profound truth in mysticism, and if they do belong together it is perfectly natural that man should know God when their lives come in contact. God and man are not insulated personalities. It should require no supernatural ecstasy, no destruction of normal faculties, no transcendence of the human, for them to meet. Sin is the only separator, the only veil. Remove this, and there is no gulf to be spanned.

There is, too, no proper schism between the mind and the heart. They can no more be sundered than a living child can be divided into two living parts. Intellect and emotions are not two independent faculties. Mind does not go to a certain distance after truth and then turn the search over to something above mind.

> " Mind and soul according well,
> *Shall* make one music as before,
> But vaster."

So, too, they are wrong who divide the universe into a dualism of natural and supernatural—the supernatural beginning where the natural leaves off.

The moment God is shut out of any part of this universe and is confined to a circle which only touches or bisects the natural realm we have an irrational universe, and our search for truth is blocked hopelessly. No, this whole cosmic system is God's and it is all from outer rim to inner core stuff which can be transmuted into spiritual meaning and which has a use for spiritual beings— because, as our greatest and healthiest mystic has seen, "God is all and in all," and "in Him all things consist." We are spiritual and partakers of spiritual truth—not because we have suppressed our human faculties and been caught up into a remote heaven, but because "He is our life." This life is completed by this mystic union with God, but this union with Him is conditional upon a union with our brethren in a complete spiritual organism— "That they may be one, as we are one."

THE MESSAGE OF EARLY QUAKERISM.

IV.

THE MESSAGE OF EARLY QUAKERISM.

EVERY great movement in the world embodies an idea. It often happens that those who are working out the idea are only dimly conscious of its full meaning, but yet it gives direction and form to the whole process, and if we wish to understand the movement, we must first hunt down the *idea*. The great religious movement of the seventeenth century, which is called Quakerism, is no exception. It has its fundamental principle which throws light upon, if it does not explain, all the peculiarities of this so-called revival of primitive Christianity.

In a certain rough and general way religions may be divided into two classes, those which have an aim and purpose to change the attitude and disposition of God toward men, and secondly, those which deal primarily with the disposition, the character, the inner nature of the human soul and its attitude toward God. In religions of the first class priests are essential and sacrifice and ritual become an elemental part of worship. In the second, the whole problem becomes a personal one : How to get a transformed and sanctified nature, how to realise the potential self, how to perfect the being. The supreme question for the first is, How can we get God to *account* us righteous and how can we escape the consequences of wrong-doing ? For the second it is, How can we become righteous and avoid sin ? For the first, the church and its rites and ceremonies, its creeds and its prayers, are a good, as an end in themselves ; for the second, nothing is a good in itself, except a glorified nature, a rightly fashioned will, and a pure and loving heart.

George Fox, who is the original exponent of Quakerism, could find no satisfaction for himself in the peculiar performances which in his day largely constituted religion. The whole system appeared foreign to his needs. It did not materially contribute to the end, which for him from very early life was the supreme one, the attainment of inward harmony and peace through deliverance from sin. He felt that there was no correspondence between the religious system of the church and the supreme purpose of life. No amount of faithfulness to the one produced the other. It was the clear conviction that the church of his day had no " open sesame " to the life which alone could satisfy his nature that drove him into a profound melancholy and made him a solitary seeker for another way, if peradventure there were any other way. The " hollow casks," as he called the ministers to whom he went for light, had no single word to give him. They could not understand in the first place what the young

man really wanted. It was a new idea that anybody should want a real face back of the picture,
when for them the picture *was* the face. Why
should he plague his head over any other reality
than this shadow which satisfied all ordinary men?
But it was just that reality other than the shadow
which the young man felt he must have. Shadow
raised to the *nth* power was for him shadow
still. He would have substance or nothing. The
real difficulty was that he wanted to find God,
and no person could give him any method which
furthered his quest ; all known trails merely led to
where God had been *once.* Here was a book
which told how God once expressed Himself
directly to men, even took flesh and tabernacled
among them. But the Book only told of divine
historic facts, which were now glorious memories,
that made the present silence all the harder to
bear. Here was a church which had a divine
origin. Far off at its source God had wrought
and the first building stones had been laid by
divine hands, but the link with that divine Personality was the shadowy touch of a succession
of consecrated hands. Here was a system of
theology which was supposed to express the
divine thought and preserve it unchanged through
the ages, but the very central feature of it was a
dead Christ and nowhere in it could he find the
present God he sought—only at the most some
exact and careful language about Him. These are
all things which a person might accept and assent

to and still remain in sin and be as far from a soul's peace as ever. He has as yet found no reconstructive principle which puts the whole life on a new level. Such a principle does, however, come to him in a "revelation" as an "opening," like a flash out of the sky. This principle may be summed up in his discovery, that religion must begin as a divine life within a man. "All believers," he would say, "must be born of God, pass from death to life, and none others are true believers but such." It means, of course, that salvation is an actual change in the man's life. His next step is the discovery that Christ is no dead Christ but a living one, still present and able to "speak to one's condition." He saw now that this very restlessness and hunger for truth which he had experienced in the years of search were proof of the infinite goodness of God, who had never left him, who had disturbed his ease as the mother-bird disturbs the nest that the young may learn to fly. But there is more involved than this : Christ, and so God Himself, is found right here within and not somewhere else. It is no longer the old disappointing story that He was somewhere once, but disappeared. We have the glorious fact announced, "Behold He is here now and I have found Him," and this is the key to the whole Quaker message. The same God who said "Let there be light," who shaped the course of the Hebrew commonwealth, who led His prophets to the mount of vision, who dwelt among

men in Jesus Christ and so manifested His glory
and His love—that same God is so near that the
heart that wants Him finds Him, the soul that
listens for Him hears Him and the person who
obeys Him and trusts Him becomes born into His
life, and so begins a new life which at its source
is divine, and may in time crowd the old life completely out. It will be seen at once that we are
here dealing with a religion of, what we called,
the second type. It begins in a purpose to find
God, it ends with a conscious likeness to Him. " I
was taken up," says George Fox, " in the love of
God, so that I could not but admire the greatness
of His love ; and while I was in that condition it
was opened unto me by the eternal light and
power, and I therein clearly saw, that all was
done and to be done, in and by Christ." " Christ,"
he says again, "it was who had enlightened me,
that gave me His light to believe in and gave me
hope which is in Himself, revealed Himself in me
and gave me His spirit."

George Fox variously calls his newly discovered
principle "the Christ within," "the inner light"
and the "seed." It means in any case that a man
becomes truly religious when he becomes aware
that there is a divine Being within the reach of
his own consciousness, *i.e.*, that the self and God
are not wholly foreign to each other. It means
that religion is fundamentally a life and a growth,
and that this life, which produces a "new creature," is the divine Being taking root, so to speak,

and growing within the human soul. This life becomes light, and the soul thereby becomes sensitive to good and evil and is made capable of free choices of the right. It is a veritable divine life forming within so that the old self yields place to a spiritual self. It becomes the Christian ideal to have the spirit and life of God in the heart— the Christ within. This is no new idea with George Fox, as everybody knows; it is the beginning and ending of the original Gospel—the "good news" that there is something so close and intimate between humanity and Divinity that God can express Himself in human terms—even in human form—and that man—any man—who receives Him can become like Him, and further, that life on its very highest level is nothing less than living a life in the flesh which reproduces in measure and degree that perfect typical God-man life. George Fox takes it all literally, and goes to work to realise it in himself and to call all other men to it. "I saw the blood of the new covenant, how it came into the heart." "The Lord opened to me how every man was enlightened by the divine light of Christ." "I knew God by revelation as He who hath the key did open, and as the Father of life drew me to His Son by His spirit." These words mean that religion, at least with this man, is first of all an inward, personal experience. The blood of the covenant is not merely a theological dogma, it is not a metaphysical theory to be held and preached about alone. Out from the heart the new life must spring and all that blood means or can mean must be grasped, not in a doctrine, but as a fact of the life. The very life-principle, which the blood symbolises, which was in the Saviour of men, must become the principle of the Christian's life and must pulsate from his heart through every fibre of his being. So, too, with the light. It means hardly more or less than a self-demonstration through the spirit of a relationship with God, which, through obedience, becomes clearer and more expansive, until the things of the Spirit attest themselves and prove their reality, as to the experienced mathematician the figures and laws of empty space become more sure even than the temporal, tangible world.

As Kant finds the form of an eternal moral law written in the very structure of the being, which says to every man, "thou must," so the Quaker says that there is a law of the heart, a divine light in the soul, "that of God," as he calls it, which is absent from no sane man. It may, only too easily, be disobeyed, shut round with our own darkness and lost to use as the diamond in the dirt. Browning, who held substantially the same truth, says : "The child feels God a moment,*ichors o'er the place, plays on and grows to be a man like us." But Fox believes still further that this so-called "light," this "voice," this "law," this "seed" is the living Christ, the Holy Spirit coming into immediate relations with us, and working out, as we co-operate, our salvation ; as the principle

* To "*ichor* o'er the place " is an illustration taken from physiology. The formation of a cicatrix over a flesh wound is the ichoring over the spot. So the child becomes case-hardened after the first effect of the Divine touch and the sensitive soul grows callous *i.e, ichored.*

of life works within the growing plant. The question at once arises, as it did in an earlier day, what place does this leave for the Scriptures and for the historic basis of Christianity, if every man may enjoy a light in his own soul, if every man may be taught directly, and if salvation is a work of the Divine Spirit bringing transformation and newness of life to all who co-operate with Him? This problem hardly presented itself to George Fox. Like the happy child who enjoys his mother's love too much to ask how such unselfish love is consistent with the law of individual struggle for existence, he is too sure of direct alliance with God to ask how this is to be reconciled with certain historical theories. It is possible, however, to suggest how he would answer the question : "God has always been talking to men," he would say, "as far as they have been ready and willing to listen to Him and capable of understanding Him. The very crudest religion of the untutored savage is indication of a light, however feeble and dim ; the very distinction of right and wrong, however imperfect the standard, is evidence of a budding principle which could not originate in a mere clay image, a man of mere carnal nature. This vision, which is so dim and shadowy in most men, may become unclouded sight in those rare souls who have been purified and refined and made holy and spiritual by bringing their lives into complete parallelism with the divine purposes. Through such holy men God has

spoken. The messages which have come through
them have a permanent value and are profitable
for the spiritual life of all ages. But these writings
—called Scriptures—have a meaning and spiritual
significance to us only because we partake of the
same Spirit as did those men who were moved to
write them. They are not to take the *place* of the
Spirit, they only show us how the Spirit manifests
Himself when He has a perfectly responsive
instrument ; and so they become the standard of
revelation. In no sense do they do away with the
necessity for a present immediate communion with
God or for a personal revelation of God in the
soul, or do they preclude the search for further
truth which God may reveal in these or any other
times. They simply stand as the high water mark
of God's revelation through men. The proper
Christian must see them as the master literature of
the Spirit of God, but he is not shut up to this
Book alone—to spell out as with fingers of the
blind the words which God once wrote before He
ceased to speak to us. Each Christian must live
in the Spirit which gave forth these Scriptures, and
so only can he authenticate them, understand them,
and use them." Those who know their Fox's
Journal and Barclay's Apology will recognise that
I have summed up the spirit of their teaching on
this subject. In regard to the historic basis of
Christianity, it may be said that the early Friends
took practically the same position which the
Apostle Paul took. The earthly life of Christ was

to them a fact of supreme importance. It was the culmination of the manifestation of the self-revealing God. It showed once for all what God was like and what He would do to bring men to Him. The real purpose of His coming was to make men like Himself, not to enact a divine drama as a spectacle. In order to make men like Himself, He had completely to reveal Himself, and then to give such a mighty motive and spiritual impulse as should move men forever to Himself. Both Paul and Fox find *that* in the Cross of Christ. " He loved me and gave Himself for me," therefore, "the life I now live in the flesh I live by the faith of the Son of God." Fox takes the Incarnation literally, as "God with us," but he finds in it the further fact that this same Christ who became a sinless Personality is striving to win all lives and to reproduce Himself in men. " They asked me," he says, " whether I was sanctified. I answered, Yes ; for I was in the paradise of God. Then they asked me if I had no sin. I answered that Christ my Saviour had taken away my sin ; and in Him is no sin. They asked how we knew that Christ did abide in us ? I said by His spirit that He hath given us. They temptingly asked if any of us were Christ. I answered, Nay we were nothing. Christ was all. They said, If a man steal is it no sin ? I answered, All unrighteousness is sin."

This leads us to the phase of the Quaker message which is sometimes called perfectionism or sanctification. This idea of a victorious and triumphant life is involved in the very essence of the message and cannot be divorced from it. His great contemporary, Bunyan, expresses a type of religion which is in decided contrast to this idea. The "Christian" of the "Progress" is probably a correct picture of the ordinary Christian, but it is a type which Fox's whole life is bent on proving a false type. "Christian" wants to escape hell, he wishes to get rid of a burden on his back. But he is never sure of himself. He loses his roll and has to go back after it, he yields to Giant Despair and lies down in the dungeon of Doubting Castle. He just manages to get along over the difficulties by the constant help and stimulus of his valiant and courageous friends, but the real shout of victory is heard only when the last deep water has been passed and heaven's gate opens. The Quaker's whole struggle is to get freed from sin and to live a *present* life in the power of God. The "Holy Grail" of his quest is nothing short of a redeemed nature and a victorious spiritual life to be realised as a demonstrated fact. That he meant by perfection, or sanctification, incapacity or inability to sin, he nowhere says, and such a view is inconsistent with what he does say. He could not, furthermore, have meant that he had attained to the goal and limit of spiritual progress. He merely meant that he had been delivered from the power of sin and the love of it, and was living instead in the power of Christ. He believed that so long as he continued to live in this power of Christ, sin was foreign to him, impossible in fact for him, and that in this same power lay the possibility of apprehending the full measure of life in Christ. This, or something quite like it, is the seed principle of Quakerism. We have put it into the language of our own time, but we believe we have not distorted it.

It remains to see how the principle applies itself and how it explains some of the peculiarities which attach to our history. It must be recognised at once that it is a method of reformation, of reconstruction, of regeneration for individuals and for society. In fact, the apostles of Quakerism profoundly believed that they had a principle which would transform society and make "this world another world." They believed that their ideal would become a universal reality and would reconstruct human society as Newton's law of gravitation had reconstructed all conceptions of the universe. They went out to call men to strict obedience to the divine Voice wherever it spoke. There is no better illustration of the effect of faith. So long as this high faith lasted, no country was too remote, no labour too hard, no call too high, no prison too horrible to daunt the Quaker with his message. The greatest statesman, even Oliver himself, and the meanest politician with his paltry scheme, were called to govern according to the divine Voice. "I did admonish him [Oliver Cromwell] to harken to God's voice, that he might stand in his counsel and obey it." This same principle was to be applied to every conceivable business and profession of life. "Mind the leading of God." "Your teacher is within you, obey him." "Mind that in thee which doth convince thee." This was to be the rule and test for all actions however simple and unimportant until this law within should be obeyed as naturally as the law of gravitation now is. This of course made the Quaker a reformer of evil customs of every sort. He came into history during a great civil war, and he saw at once that war was a wicked custom, inconsistent at every point with the religion which he illustrated. He settled his position by saying that he lived "in virtue of that life and power which does away with the occasion for all war." It was his mission, not to cry against war in the abstract, but to live himself in "this life and power" and to bring, as far as it lay in his ability, all other men into it, and so to produce a society in which war would be impossible. He became an uncompromising opponent of injustice in the courts, of corruption and tyranny in the administration of law, of arbitrary methods in government, not simply because he himself suffered from such abuses, but really because his principle was at stake. According to this principle, every man *is a man* and has a man's rights. In other words, the divine right of man is superior to the divine right of kings. The judge and the king must be called back to observe "that of God within them" as much as the poorest peasant, and the man who rules or judges by a selfish or arbitrary method is out of accord with the divine nature of things and must be testified against at all costs, for this principle of the divine right of man is at stake.

It is his adherence to what I have called the divine right of man that constitutes the Quaker's sense of human equality. He was not a " leveller " --except as he wanted to level everybody up to the highest. He knew that men were differently endowed and equipped, and that they could not be reduced to a lot of equal atoms of human society. What he meant was that every man had a right to be a man, and to work out his manhood under the divine leading. That whether low or high each human being has a self to realise for which he is responsible to God, and that nothing must prevent him from exercising his functions as a free spiritual man. The man is more than raiment and he must not become a creature of fashion, a peg to hang clothes upon. The personality must govern dress, not dress the personality. This worth and dignity of man—of all men—must, the Quaker held, be everywhere emphasised, therefore hollow custom and sham manners in every walk of life must cease. A man is a man, and he shall be treated as one. There is much in the garb-question and " hat honour " and " singular " address and absence of title—even of Mr.—which strikes us to-day as rather petty and foolish, an overdrawn distinction. That may be so, but it was occasioned by the Quaker's resolve to be absolutely honest, and to fight sham, as the mythical Hercules fought beasts, and overdrawn or not, this scrupulous determination to be as honest and straightforward before man as before God has done much to clear the air of sham and to crack the husk of the foolish customs.

But a much greater issue than this is involved in the Quaker's conception of man and his relation to God. Let it be remembered that our fundamental principle is, that each man has direct relation and dealings with God. If he is saved, it must be through his own choice, not by the act of another. Within the circle of his own life stands a sanctuary of which he alone is the priest. If God is met there, it is because he meets Him; if God's voice is heard and obeyed, he is the one who hears it; if sins are forgiven it is not through another that it is known, but by the forgiven soul itself. Therefore, all that is absolutely necessary for divine worship, or service, is a human being —any devout human being—with an open heart toward God. A man and God, met together, make a holy place, and this meeting constitutes worship. The vocal expression is not the important thing— it is the real meeting of the soul with God that is all-important. It is a fact that such meeting is rendered easier where many kindred spirits meet with one accord than where one individual sits alone, and this is one reason for public meetings for worship. Another reason, and perhaps the main one, for public meetings, is the fact that some persons are more capable of appreciating and apprehending divine truth than others are. It becomes thus the duty and privilege of those who see, to interpret to those who do not see so clearly. This ability to minister is a gift which consists first in the power to see, and secondly in the power to impart the truth in its relation to the spiritual needs of men. The minister, of course, can do nothing for the congregation apart from their co-operation. He does not act or speak or pray *for* them. He is merely one man among them who is gifted with rare spiritual sight and whose sole function is to help others *see*. Every office or position in the church rests on the same principle, for the Quaker. No magical authority attaches to any position. The weight of the official person rests solely on his spiritual capacity and his ability to perform the functions which devolve upon him. It is after all only a man, doing some particular work for which the Lord has fitted him.

The Quaker needs to say little of the so-called ordinances, for there is no more place for them in his conception of Christianity than there is for horses on an electric car. They fall off as the old leaves do when the new ones come. It is an essential feature of Quakerism that the individual Christian communes with God and feeds his spiritual life by partaking of the living Christ who nourishes the whole inner being. If this is so in fact, what place is left for bread and wine, which at best could only be a symbol of what he already has in reality? If it is true that the believer enters consciously into the divine life, *i.e.*, is baptised into Christ and puts on Christ, what place is left for the use of water, which at best could only symbolise what he already has *in fact*. Furthermore, the use of material things to produce a spiritual effect seems to him from the nature of the case unwarrantable. He fails further to find any clear and unmistakeable command from the Master for the institution of a system of things which seems to him incompatible with the whole spirit of the Gospel, and he concludes that if they ever had a place in the church it could only have been while it was in its Jewish swaddling clothes. In short, he finds no justification for *any* system or practice which becomes a substitute for the Spirit Himself, or which lessens the positive aspiration of the soul to find God Himself and to live in Him.

This virile and constructive interpretation of Christianity which we find in the message of the early Friends should have deeply affected the course of religious thought and profoundly influenced the development of society and the race. It has in it the seed of a new life and a new society and a new state. It has not yet realised its promise. In fact, the truth of its real message has never mastered even the little group of men and women who have borne the name—"Friends." The idea which lies at the root has never had an adequate embodiment. It has found great individual exponents and interpreters, but no full corporate expression. George Fox himself is the best possible exemplification of the Quaker idea of a man with his life in parallelism with divine currents—fearless, tireless, active, practical, and with all, aware in his very soul that his life is linked in union with the divine life and that his main business as a man is to become an instrument for God.

William Penn patiently endeavoured to work out in his western commonwealth the Quaker principles as applied to the state—and it was his purpose to found a state—not in Utopia, but in Pennsylvania —where the people should make their own laws, hold their own religious views, follow the voice within, where justice should be given to everybody, high or low, rich or poor, white or brown, where all should be educated, where all should be free to realise their potential lives and to become what God meant them to be, and where war should be unknown. All that one brave and noble man could do to make the "holy experiment" a realised fact Penn did, but he did not and he could not lift the mass of his followers to the high level of his own conception. It is the holy experiment of William Penn rather than of the Society of Friends.

Robert Barclay, the young scholar of the movement, grasped in a marvellous way the central features and implications of the Quaker principle and expressed them with convincing argument and unanswerable logic. But his book—though in some

periods and localities treated almost as a fetish—
has exerted surprisingly little influence. More than
half the Friends in the world do not know what
is in it, and hold the very views which this book
combats so successfully ; while the most of those
who have been quoting it all their lives have never
once seen the bearing of this book on the onward
movement of religious thought, nor how it put the
Quaker in a position to have led the Christian
church in search for Truth. Barclay has been
either ignored or read microscopically. He has
not been interpreted by his people or to his
people, certainly not to the world.

It is not our purpose now to tell why Quakerism
has not been more effective in the world than it
has been. We are for the moment dealing with
its primitive message, and so far as we can now
grasp it, it has a universal element in it. In fact,
it is as ancient as the first century and as modern
as the twentieth. It is not "new theology," but it
expresses that permanent truth that God by His
Spirit is working all things up to better, that His
purpose is to make men into His own image and
to reveal His life, light, truth and love in every
man who will respond to Him and fulfil the conditions of spiritual life. It is a contribution to the
world's knowledge of the divine method of the
making of man—the man who possesses the power
of an endless life, and if it ever does get adequate
expression in an organic body it will have a
mighty transforming power on the world.

THE STRONGHOLD OF THE FAITH.

V.

THE STRONGHOLD OF THE FAITH.

THERE is a widely accepted theory that the true religion is forever fixed and unchangeable. It is a system of doctrine, mysteriously communicated, not to be questioned by reason, to be accepted by faith, and to be guarded as a "deposit" of truth, crystallised into a form suited to every age and every race of men. If this were so, we should have nothing to do but to accept the deposit of truth, as the South Sea Islander accepts the breadfruit which gravitation brings to his lap. We should have a fixed standard by which to test every idea, as we now test our clocks by the Washington observatory, and error would simply be deviation from this standard. This deposit of truth, this body of doctrine would be the stronghold of the faith. It would be our Mount Olympus, our supremely sacred citadel, but if it ever should be carried by the enemy there would be no second hill, no other kopje, in which we could entrench ourselves. There are, however, fatal objections to this theory. In the first place, there is no such fixed and unchangeable deposit of doctrine. History shows truth in process, never crystallised. It is always *being* revealed and apprehended— never a finished fact. There is nothing in the world which is so absolutely unmistakeable and clear that it can be used as the foot-rule of truth and error to test every idea by. Then, too, from the very nature of truth it could not be crystal- lised and fixed into something hard and fast. Truth is not of the nature of some food product which can be canned or preserved, or put into capsules. Like goodness or virtue, it belongs to a life—or better still, it *is* a life, which means, of course, that it can no more be reduced to an abstract statement, and so be preserved, than a flower can be pressed in an herbarium and still remain a flower. Truth lives and grows and sweeps on in wider circles. It expresses itself in myriad forms, as life always does, it is an eternal process of manifestation, and it can no more be caught and deposited than the motion of a spinning top can.

But even if there were an absolute standard of truth in the world which could not be questioned, and even if truth could be captured and put into fixed and rigid form for all time, it would not meet the needs of human souls. The men who are fed by gravitation from the bread-fruit tree are incomparably lower than the men who tease the hard and stubborn soil of the New England farms to produce for them the necessities of life. The bread eaten in the sweat of the brow makes the sturdy, independent manhood, and nature is not kind to us when she pours out her bounties so that we may forego the struggle. Truth received as a deposit and put into the passive mind would have a still more disastrous effect. The mind never was, and never can be, a receptacle. It grows and expands by free choices, by perceiving and discovering truth for itself, by reaching and stretching beyond what it has to what lies before it, by painfully toiling and struggling to follow the stream up to its source, and by making itself an organ or instrument of the truth.

But even if the mind could assimilate truth fed to it in crystallised form, still this method would reduce us all to one flat, dead level of attainment. A communism of property is questionable enough, but such a communism of thought is more serious still. Each soul takes his share of truth and then is pledged not to add to it or subtract from it. It ends in producing a race of men no more original than a quartz crystal, and the human mind becomes only a static vessel to hold its quota of the whole stock of truth. Whenever a nation has tried to maintain and enforce this conception of truth its vitality has dried up, its originality has ceased, its creative activity has slackened, its moral fibre has weakened and degeneration has become only too apparent.

We do not hesitate, then, to pronounce this theory discredited by facts and at variance with the whole spirit of the original Christian message.

There is no sure stronghold of faith, *unless* the God who spoke once is speaking still, and unless revelation is a continuous process. If there is no relation at all between the human soul and God, and if we have no means of direct vision, no capacity for truth at first hand, we can have no permanent assurance that the truth which men of old time saw was really grounded in the nature of things and that it will abide. Our supposed island may any day turn out to be, as in the Arabian story, a moving sea-monster. No, our real test and assurance of past truth and of former revelation is to be found in the fact that God still speaks to us to-day, that human souls are not isolated from God and that we are immediately conscious of truths which form a necessary part of the eternal process of truth, which has its source in God. We know we are alive because our consciousness of the moment links on with our whole past existence, and we know that this past existence belongs to us because we feel its unity with our present life. But the man who should lose his consciousness of the moment would lose at the same time all sense of past existence. So also our sense of the worth of revelation, the reality of the truth which has been, rests for us upon our assurance of a present God who reveals Himself, and upon our present consciousness that we know the truth when it comes to us. We feel ourselves a part of the entire process of truth, as each bubble might feel itself a part of the whole river which moves on to the ocean from which it first rose. We must therefore seek for our stronghold of faith, as we sought for our basis of faith, not somewhere outside of man's life—not in some middle third thing between God and man—but in man himself and in his relation to God.

We have come at last to see, if we are Christians, that God is self-revealing, that it belongs to His very nature and essence to show Himself, *i.e.*, He could not be God and stay self-contained and self-regarding. This is the first fact of the Christian religion, and it is a fact which is grounded in the divine nature. There is a second fact which is grounded in *human* nature, and that is that man has a capacity for knowing God *when* He reveals Himself, *i.e.*, that truth is self-demonstrative when it comes to us. There is no other proof that the sun is shining except this, that we see and feel it. There is no foreign evidence that love is of supreme worth—nothing except the heart's own testimony. There is no other proof that there is beauty in the world than this, that we perceive it and that our hearts beat with joy at it. It is just this same "demonstration of the spirit" which is the unassailable stronghold of faith—the citadel of religion. Light shines in vain for blind fishes in the cave, beauty has no meaning for the eye devoid of "speculation," love is only a word for the heart which has never felt it. Religion could not be—even with a self-revealing God—if we could not know Him when He spoke, if we could not see Him when He showed Himself, if we could not feel Him when He touched us.

Paul is right, therefore, in staking his case on "the demonstration of the spirit," the witness within the consciousness of the believer. This means that religion is something which can be as thoroughly and practically tested as any facts in the universe. We know of an external world only because it stands revealed in our consciousness and because we trust in the reality of what appears to us. Our law of right or of duty is a law which we discover in the structure of our own being and which we obey because we feel an obligation—an oughtness—from which we cannot alienate ourselves. We feel the power of ideals toward which we move, not because we see a definite goal standing before us, but because we feel within ourselves the law of the fuller life which we are to realise. Not otherwise are God and all the truths of religion made known and certified. It is the kind of evidence an artist has of beauty when he stands caught by the glory of a sunset. It is the kind of evidence of the laws of mathematics which an astronomer has when a new planet appears just where his calculations said it must be ; it is the kind of evidence an experimenter has of the power of electricity when the current from the dynamo thrills through him to the ends of his fingers and to the roots of his hair.

A religion which builds on authority or on the deposits of tradition stands securely only so long

as the "authority" can defy investigation or can
maintain itself in the face of investigation.   It
contains in itself no inherent prophecy of a date-
less future.   The gods of Olympus hold their sway
there only till the mountain is climbed.   On the
other hand, the religion which witnesses itself to
the soul, which bases itself in the experience of
the heart, which stops not short of a demonstration
of the spirit, need fear no investigation, is as
certain as self-existence is, and has in itself a
prophecy of a period co-eternal with the revealing
God.

The strength of modern science lies in the fact
that every law which it announces, everything it
proclaims, is tested at once by facts.   It holds to
nothing which will not square with the nature of
things.   Every department of science is strewn
with the wrecks of discarded theories, untenable
hypotheses and rejected "laws," rejected because
they failed to square with facts.   Nothing abides
in science which cannot stand every possible test
of facts, while that which is plumb with the nature
of things is permanent.   I have in these papers
been declaring a religion which in the same way
meets every conceivable test.   It is the religion of
fact, of life, of experience.   We believe in God
not because some remote race had dealings with
Him, not merely because some sacred books tell
of Him, not because an authoritative church or a
dogmatic theology proclaims Him.   All these things
may well add to and strengthen our faith, may

properly carry conviction to our hearts; but we believe in God primarily because we ourselves find Him, because we cannot flee or hide from Him if we would, because we have our being in Him, and because the moment we act as though He were present by our side we find that He really is there. He is involved in all our thinking and in all our doing and when we in blindness say, "Show us the Father," He patiently answers, "Have I been so long with thee and yet hast thou not known me?" The soul that cannot find God in his own life and who gets no hint of His presence now, would surely have some difficulty in proving the reality of His presence in Hebrew history, but on the other hand, the soul that realises that his life is immediately grounded in God and that the one sure fact of consciousness is the reality of the Divine self, has a sure basis for his faith in the reality of God's presence with "them of old time." The reality of the inspiration of the writers of the Scriptures is demonstrated in the same way. They exert a power over our lives and they carry conviction to our hearts not because they are canonical, not because they are backed by supernatural authority, but because they appeal to us, speak to our lives, reveal things which our deepest nature feels to be true. Coleridge used to say, "I believe in the Bible because it finds me." These writings exercise a spiritual power over our lives, because they come from men who have had profounder and loftier experiences and visions of

our God and His truth than we have, and yet our
own experiences of God prepare us to rise to the
significance and meaning of these master-revela-
tions. They carry us and win us not because they
are unlike anything we know, but rather because
they are the highest level of divine-human relation,
lower levels of which we already know in ourselves. We shall not prove their authenticity by
an appeal to miracle, or by some celestial mark
upon them, or by the decision of an infallible
council which made the canon, but rather by
showing, as we can, that they are profitable for
the formation of spiritual lives and saintly character ; that they show forth our God and His
purpose and that they are sources of present
inspiration to those who go down into their meaning. The supreme test of the Scriptures is the
practical one of their power over us when we use
them rightly. If they can stand that test they
need fear no other ; and if they cannot, no dogmatic assertion about them can save them. The
stronghold of our faith in them is the fact that
our hearts *do* feel their power and that they are
dynamic in the making of spiritual lives. We
begin with an experiment and end with an experience. Every new test of their value increases
our conviction of inspiration until we become so
sure that we want no other proof of it any more
than we want proof of our mother's love beyond
the love itself !

The same method and test apply to every one

of our Christian doctrines. They are not true
because they are in ancient creeds, they are not
true because ministers and churches dogmatically
declare them. They rest on no foundation which
may cave in any day. They are true, if they *are*
true, because they are supreme facts of life—of
spiritual life—and because they abide the deepest
tests of life.

The Christian revelation of God demonstrates
itself to us as the light demonstrates itself to all
who have a sensitive retina. It comes to us as
light and moisture come to a flower, which prove
their value and worth by putting themselves into
the life of the flower. Abstract theories of Christ's
nature are wide the mark for religion, and are no
more necessary to salvation than abstract theories
on any other subject. We must, again, approach
Christ and the Christian doctrines with our tests
of experience. What does He claim to be? What
does He claim to do? He claims—these are His
supreme claims—to manifest God, and to put man
into relationship with Him—to make him a son of
God with a likeness to the Father. Well, we are
brought back at once to the undeniable fact that
we cannot think now of God except in terms of
Christ's revelation of Him. Climb as high as ever
we will, we discover that Christ is ahead of us.
We call God spirit, but He first so revealed Him.
We say He is love, but He showed Him to *be*
love. We say God is Light and Truth, but this
also comes through Him who said " I am the

Light and the Truth." "The God and Father of
our Lord Jesus Christ" is the God our souls long
for, the God who meets our highest aspirations,
who seals Himself as the goal of all other revelations and who is witnessed to by that "the likest
God within the soul."

But the real test comes when we try the other
claim, for here at least we are on no alien ground.
He himself claims to prove His divinity by making
us sons of God. We are to believe not simply
because He said "Rise up and walk," not because
He said "Come forth," not even because He said
to Thomas, after three days in the grave, "Reach
hither thy finger and feel the prints of the nails."
We are to believe because we can test the power
of His life in our lives and because we can see
whether His highest claim is true. He professes
to be able to take a man who has lived in sin,
who has been self-centred and absorbed in self,
who has borne all the marks of the earthly, and
given no promise of the heavenly life, and to
transform him into a being of the spiritual order,
glowing with love, forgetful of self, dying to live,
and living to do the will of another, and with a
life in parallelism with the divine purpose. In
short, He claims to be able to impart the divine
life to men, to spiritualise and transform their
lives. It is a claim which can be as carefully
tested as the law of gravitation can. How do you
know there is such a law? You see every particle
of matter in the universe obey it. It swings satel-

lites and planets and by it you can calculate their motions and positions. It draws the whole ocean and dashes it twice a day high up the beach and you can announce weeks before the exact moment of flood tide. How do we know that Jesus Christ is the Power of God unto salvation and that God's love comes through Him to us? There is one sure test. Try Him. Turn your face to Christ, obey every call from Him, make an experiment of following Him completely, trust Him as you trust the laws of nature, throw yourself upon Him in absolute confidence, act as though you saw Him standing by you. The result will be—the testimony is universal—you will find a new creation going on within. The old nature will go as the ghostly leaves of winter go when the new buds open. The new nature will come as "noiselessly as the springtime her crown of verdure weaves." New avenues of activity will open, life will become richer, the reality of God will stand no more in theory, heaven will not seem some far off terminus, and God's will will cease to be some stubborn objective law; it will become an inward choice and pleasure. Such a Christianity has a three-fold demonstration: its effect on other individuals, its effect on our own personal lives, and its transforming effect on society. No one who has ever seen a saint made by the power of God in Jesus Christ can doubt that there is something dynamic in such a religion. One may doubt the truth of transubstantiation, or question the value of outward baptism, but he knows that only a spiritual power can change hate to love, sullenness to sweetness, harshness to gentleness, impulsiveness to calm patience, and fretful discouragement to confidence and victory.

Then comes the first-hand evidence in one's own life. There can be no proof so convincing as the fact that He has drawn *me* out of the horrible pit and the miry clay. He has established *my* goings and put a new song in *my* mouth. We know that we are of God because we love, because we have the witness, because we overcome, because God has brought us up into His life. Then there is that slow but steady coming of the kingdom, going on before the eyes of those who can see— the propagation of the divine life through the world. " The dial plate marks centuries with the minute finger." It seems like the slow swing of the globe in the procession of the equinoxes which in a thousand years give us a new pole star. But though slow, like the motion of the glacier, the movement of God in history toward " one far off divine event" is unmistakeable and irresistible. The old corrupt order *does* change, the relics of a pagan age are weeded out, the entrenched evils of centuries finally do yield. New revelations come, prophets appear, the horizon of light enlarges. Men become more civilised, more humanised, more spiritualised, more Christlike. The New Jerusalem is something more than a dream because God is at work in His world and when we take long perspectives we trace His hand. "There is a serene Providence," our Emerson says, "which rules the fate of nations, which makes little account of time, little of one generation or race, makes no account of disasters, conquers alike by what is called defeat and by what is called victory, thrusts aside enemy and obstruction, crushes everything immoral as inhuman, and obtains the ultimate triumph of the best race by the sacrifice of everything which resists the moral laws of the world. It makes its own instruments, creates the man for the time, trains him in poverty, inspires his genius and arms him for his task." (Emerson's "Abraham Lincoln.")

The moment we begin to live by a Christianity which declares that God is not afar, but in every spiritual fact and process of life and history, that He is manifesting Himself in every victory over sin, in every defeat of evil and march of righteousness, in every soul that puts on the white robe and takes the palm-branch—in short, when we build on the truth of a present God who witnesses to Himself in us and proves His power as light does and as love and beauty do, we need never be afraid of losing Him or of losing anything which really shows Him forth. In this stronghold of faith which tests itself by spiritual facts, we can meet all the questions, the doubts, the scepticism of our time, and we can positively establish our truth. The new conclusions of science do not weaken one single point of support under such a faith. Has man come up by a process of evolution from lower forms of life ?   Well, if such a view is established, we simply get a new idea of the divine method of creation, for a universe in endless process presupposes God as much as a world finished at a stroke does.   We cannot understand why there should ever be sin in a world turned out perfect from the finger of God.   But we see that there must be sin and evil and imperfection in a world which is still only in process of making. In our old system of thought the origin of sin implies a defeat of God which could be remedied only through an elaborate *scheme* of redemption. If this new idea is true, God never has been defeated.   His upward purpose has simply been growing plainer from the beginning.   His coming in an incarnation was no afterthought, no scheme. It was part of the eternal process.   He shows Himself, He shows the spiritual method of drawing men up to the goal of the race.   He condemns sin, He shows its effect, He reveals love, He shows what life may be, He sets forth its type and He bestows the power for realising it.   The gospel of Christ explains the whole process.   " That is not first which is spiritual but that which is natural and afterward that which is spiritual."   At first the process is by a power working unseen from behind. Now it is by a perfect typal Personality who goes on before to draw out the man within the man. The long travail of creation has looked and pointed toward the unveiling of the Son of God.

   If we no longer look for God alone in the exceptional, the miraculous, the interventional, we on the other hand have discovered a solid basis for faith in a God who shows Himself in the whole process of the world, in the long struggle for righteousness, in the slow shaping of an ever better race, in the growing sway of love, in the victories of truth. Such a conception of religion puts it also beyond the touch of criticism, since it rests on nothing that criticism, even of the most destructive sort, can disintegrate. The relation which really exists between the soul and God, which is grounded in experience, is affected in no serious way by the discovery of new dates or new authorship for any or all the biblical books. It is immaterial whether Job or Jonah is literally historical, or dramatic, like the parables of Christ, teaching a spiritual lesson through a supposed character. Our interest lies not in maintaining some dogmatic "theory of Scripture," but in discovering the spiritual message, the practical use of these books, which so closely bear the mark and superscription of the God whom we are learning to know. We see plainly that all revelation must come in terms of the life and thought of those who receive it, and so it must be progressive. We know enough about God now to know that no conclusions of historical study can shake the foundations of religion. Much ancient theology will of necessity succumb, for theology is at the best a man-made affair, and each new century will more or less reshape the crystallised thought of former ages. But this life of God in the life of man which is the basis of religion will go steadily on. Everything which bears to the soul a genuine message of God, everything which shows Him or His purpose, will minister to that life in the future as in the past. Every book which has come out of the heart of the universe and which speaks to the heart of man will survive all tests and will continue to inspire men, regardless of its date, and wholly apart from the mere fact that this man held the pen rather than that. But we shall learn to use it not as a fetish, but as a source of spiritual light to be taken for what it is worth.

There are still harder problems than any of these. Psychology has opened a series of questions which make the boldest tremble for his faith in an endless life or in any spiritual reality. I do not need now to drag these questions to the light for examination. It is enough to say that they are deadly shots against the armour of a mediæval theology. There is, however, a basis of religion which lies wholly beyond the reach of this newest of the great sciences.

The inner spiritual life which comes into immediate relation with God, and which grows by feeding on Him, is as much a fact of consciousness as memory or perception is, and can no more be shaken than they can. This spiritual life belongs in the kingdom of ends, which even psychology has to admit, and a kingdom of ends, *i.e.*, a life of ideals and of purposes beyond the moment, involves of necessity a divine infinite self in whom we live and move and have our conscious life ; and *that* carries with it the prophecy and the potency of an endless life.

This religion of fact, this faith grounded on the soul's immediate relation with God, can meet the hardest problem that has yet appeared and can triumphantly face it. Science reduces the phenomena of the world under permanent and universal laws, so changeless and abstract that its description of facts and events, once accurately made, holds in every part of the universe for every age. But science can do nothing with the indescribable, the free, the spiritual, the ideal. These belong in another realm into which science not only does not but cannot enter. Science stops where the describable stops. Science can say with authority that a man's body is a mass of flying molecules—trillions on trillions in number—and that after a certain number of years these will fall apart and the man's bodily life will end—with no hope or promise of any reorganisation. But what can science do with the man who has so entered into the life of the risen Christ that he can say, " He hath raised us up together and made us sit together in heavenly places in Christ Jesus " ? " He hath delivered us from the power of darkness and translated us into the kingdom of His dear Son " ? " We have come to a kingdom which cannot be moved " because it is based on the interrelation of

God and man which attests itself in consciousness and is a spiritual fact?

> "A warmth within the breast would melt
> The freezing reason's colder part,
> And like a man in wrath the heart
> Stood up and answered, I have *felt*.
>
> And what I am beheld again
> What is, and no man understands,
> And out of darkness came the hands
> That reach through nature, moulding men."

CPSIA information can be obtained at www.ICGtesting.com
Printed in the USA
BVOW04s1644110913

330904BV00011B/385/P